Slip-Stitch
CAPS™

General Information

Many of the products used in this pattern book can be purchased from local craft, fabric and variety stores, or from the Annie's Attic Needlecraft Catalog (see Customer Service information on page 16).

Contents

D1299749

Introduction

These stocking caps look like they are knitted, but actually they are crocheted! They are worked in slip stitch which produces a fabric that looks and stretches like 1 x 1 knit ribbing. There is one main difference in the construction of

these caps versus knitted caps. Crocheted caps are worked up and down in rows while knitted caps are worked in the round.

Because these caps are so stretchy, one size will fit a range of head sizes. Generally a cap will stretch 3 or 4 inches, making these ideal gifts since sizing is not critical. Style affects sizing too. Right now many teens and young adults are wearing oversized caps.

BASIC CONSTRUCTION

All of the stocking caps use the same basic construction for the body of the cap. The basic stitch is slip stitch in the back loop, worked in rows. Shaping is accomplished with short rows.

One makes a short row by working only some of the stitches in the previous row and leaving the remainder unworked. These unworked stitches are then used in a later row. This forms a wedge which shapes the cap. After the body is completed, a variety of trims are added. Pompoms are optional on all the caps. Instructions for two different kinds of pompoms are given and can be interchanged or used as desired.

ADJUSTING SIZE

You can easily adjust the size of any cap by one size. You'll probably want to adjust both the circumference and the length. For the circumference, just add or subtract one pattern repeat. If you want to make the cap slightly larger or smaller, you can do a partial repeat. After the partial repeat, end with a row that goes all the way to the top of the cap to make seaming easier. For length, just add or subtract a few stitches on every row at the bottom edge of the cap.

SEAMING

These caps are worked up and down in rows, and they require one seam at the center back. You can seam them with either a crocheted slip stitch or a hand-sewn mattress stitch. The slip stitch leaves a small ridge, but is fast and doesn't require any sewing. The mattress stitch produces an invisible or nearly invisible join.

To join with slip stitch, turn after last row, bring beginning row to front of work, *insert hook in chain on opposite side of starting chain and into the back loop only of stitch on the last row, yarn over, pull through all loops on hook to complete slip stitch, repeat from * across. Fasten off.

To join with mattress stitch, leave a long strand at end of last row. With tapestry needle, match first and last rows, pass needle under chain on beginning chain and then through front and back loops of stitch on last row, repeat across row. Secure yarn. ∎

Classic Stocking Cap

SKILL LEVEL

INTERMEDIATE

FINISHED SIZE
One size fits most adults: 20-inch circumference

MATERIALS
- Moda Dea Washable Wool medium (worsted) weight yarn (3½ oz/ 166 yds/100g per ball):
    2 balls #4440 moss
- Size H/8/5mm crochet hook or size needed to obtain gauge
- Tapestry needle

4 MEDIUM

GAUGE
24 sl sts = 4 inches; 32 sl st rows = 4 inches

PATTERN NOTE
Work in **back loops** (see Stitch Guide) unless otherwise stated.

INSTRUCTIONS
CAP
Row 1: Ch 61, sl st in 2nd ch from hook and in each ch across, turn. (*60 sl sts*)

Row 2: Ch 1, sl st in each st across, leaving last 5 sts unworked for **top of Cap**, turn. (*55 sl sts*)

Row 3: Ch 1, sl st in each sl st across, turn.

Row 4: Ch 1, sl st in each st across, leaving last 5 sts unworked, turn. (*50 sl sts*)

Row 5: Ch 1, sl st in each sl st across, turn.

Row 6: Ch 1, sl st in each st across, leaving last 5 sts unworked turn. (*45 sl sts*)

Row 7: Ch 1, sl st in each sl st across, turn.

Row 8: Ch 1, sl st in each st on last row and in each unworked st across top of Cap, turn. (*60 sl sts*)

Row 9: Ch 1, sl st in each st across, turn.

Rows 10–153: [Rep rows 2–9 consecutively] 18 times.

Rows 154–160: Rep rows 2–8.

Row 161: Hold first and last rows tog, matching sts, sl st tog. Fasten off.

Weave separate strand through rows at top of Cap, pull to gather, secure end.

Fold up bottom of Cap for cuff. ∎

Corkscrew Tassel

SKILL LEVEL

INTERMEDIATE

FINISHED SIZES

Instructions given fit 13-inch head circumference (*infant*); changes for 16-inch head circumference (*toddler*) are in [ ].

MATERIALS

- Red Heart Soft Baby Steps medium (worsted) weight yarn (5 oz/ 256 yds/142g per skein):
    1 skein #9700 baby pink
- Size H/8/5mm crochet hook or size needed to obtain gauge
- Tapestry needle

GAUGE

21 sl sts = 4 inches; 28 sl st rows = 4 inches

PATTERN NOTE

Work in **back loops** (*see Stitch Guide*) unless otherwise stated.

INSTRUCTIONS

CAP

Row 1: Ch 52 [57], for **corkscrew**, 2 hdc in 3rd ch from hook and in each of next 9 chs (*first 2 chs count as first hdc*), sl st in each ch across, turn. (*40 [45] sl sts, 21 [21] hdc*)

Row [2]: For toddler size only, ch 1, sl st in each st across, leaving last 5 sl sts unworked, turn. (*[40] sl sts*)

Row [3]: Ch 1, sl st in each sl st across, turn.

Row 2 [4]: For both sizes, ch 1, sl st in each st across, leaving last 5 sl sts unworked, turn. (*35 [35] sl sts*)

4 MEDIUM

Row 3 [5]: Ch 1, sl st in each sl st across, turn.

Row 4 [6]: Ch 1, sl st in each sl st across, leaving last 5 sts unworked, turn. (*30 [30] sl sts*)

Row 5 [7]: Ch 1, sl st in each sl st across, turn.

Row 6 [8]: Ch 1, sl st in each of first 30 [30] sl sts, sl st in each of next 10 [15] unworked sl sts across top of Cap, ch 12, turn. (*40 [45] sl sts, 12 [12] chs*)

Row 7 [9]: For **corkscrew**, 2 hdc in 3rd ch from hook and in each of next 9 chs, sl st in each st across, turn. (*40 [45] sl sts, 21 [21] hdc*)

Rows 8–103 [10–113]: [Rep rows 2–7 [2–9] consecutively] 16 [13] times.

Rows 104–108 [114–120]: Rep rows 2–6 [2–8].

Row 109 [121]: Hold first and last rows tog, matching sts, sl st tog. Fasten off.

Weave separate strand through rows at base of corkscrews, pull to gather, secure end.

Fold up bottom of Cap for cuff. ■

Chullo

SKILL LEVEL

INTERMEDIATE

FINISHED SIZE

One size fits most large children and small
adults: 20-inch circumference

MATERIALS

- Moda Dea Sassy Stripes light (light
  worsted) weight yarn (1¾ oz/
  147 yds/50g per ball):
    2 balls #6946 crush
- Sizes F/5/3.75 and K/10½/6.5mm crochet
  hooks or size needed to obtain gauge
- Tapestry needle
- Stitch marker

GAUGE

Size F hook: 24 sl sts = 4 inches; 32 sl st rows =
4 inches

PATTERN NOTES

Work in **back loops** *(see Stitch Guide)* unless
otherwise stated.

Join rounds with slip stitch as indicated unless
otherwise stated.

INSTRUCTIONS
CAP

Row 1: With size F hook, ch 43, sl st in 2nd
ch from hook and in each ch across, turn.
(42 sl sts)

Row 2: Ch 1, sl st in each st across, leaving last
3 sts unworked for **top of Cap**, turn. *(39 sl sts)*

Row 3: Ch 1, sl st in each sl st across, turn.

Row 4: Ch 1, sl st in each st across, leaving last
4 sts unworked, turn. *(35 sl sts)*

Row 5: Ch 1, sl st in each st across, turn.

Row 6: Ch 1, sl st in each st across, leaving last 5 sts unworked, turn. *(30 sl sts)*

Row 7: Ch 1, sl st in each sl st across, turn.

Row 8: Ch 1, sl st in each st across, leaving last 7 sts unworked, turn. *(23 sl sts)*

Row 9: Ch 1, sl st in each sl st across, turn.

Row 10: Ch 1, sl st in each st across, leaving last 8 sts unworked, turn. *(15 sl sts)*

Row 11: Ch 1, sl st in each sl st across, turn.

Row 12: Ch 1, sl st in each st on last row and in each unworked st across top of Cap, turn. *(42 sl sts)*

Row 13: Ch 1, sl st in each st across, turn.

Rows 14–145: [Rep rows 2–13 consecutively] 11 times.

Rows 146–156: Rep rows 2–12.

Row 157: Hold first and last rows tog, matching sts, sl st tog. Fasten off.

Weave separate strand through rows at top of Cap, pull to gather and secure end.

EAR FLAP
MAKE 2.
Rnd 1: With size F hook, ch 4, **join** *(see Pattern Notes)* in beg ch to form ring, ch 1, [3 sc in ring, ch 2] 3 times, join in beg sc. *(9 sc, 3 ch sps)*

Rnd 2: Ch 1, sc in first st, 2 sc in next st, sc in next st, (sc, ch 2, sc) in next ch sp, *sc in next st, 2 sc in next st, sc in next st, (sc, ch 2, sc) in next ch sp, rep from * around, join in beg sc. *(18 sc, 3 ch sps)*

Rnds 3–6: Ch 1, sc in each st around with (sc, ch 2, sc) in each ch sp, join in beg sc. *(14 sc on each side between corner ch sps at end of last rnd)*

For **tie cord**, with size K hook, ch 53, sl st in 4th ch from hook and in each ch across, sl st in same st as last sc on Ear Flap. Fasten off.

Flatten Cap, mark each side of Cap at bottom edge, position edge of Ear Flaps opposite cord ½ inch back from markers on each side of Cap at bottom edge. Working in ends of rows between ridges, sl st around bottom edge of Cap, joining Ear Flaps to Cap where positioned *(see photo)*.

TASSEL CORD
With size K hook, join at center top of Cap, ch 13, sl st in 4th ch from hook and in each ch across, sl st in top of Cap. Fasten off.

FRINGE
For each Fringe, cut 12 strands yarn, each 6 inches long. With all strands held tog, fold in half, insert hook in ch sp, pull fold through, pull all loose ends through fold, tighten. Trim ends.

Attach 1 Fringe to ch sps at end of each Ear Flap tie cord and end of Tassel Cord at top of Cap. ∎

Beads

SKILL LEVEL

INTERMEDIATE

FINISHED SIZE
One size fits most adults: 20-inch circumference

MATERIALS
- Red Heart Designer Sport light (light worsted) weight yarn (3 oz/ 279 yds/85g per skein):
  1 skein #3301 latte
- Size F/5/3.75mm crochet hook or size needed to obtain gauge
- Tapestry needle
- Wooden large-hole 8mm beads: 171

GAUGE
21 sl sts = 4 inches; 32 sl st rows = 4 inches

PATTERN NOTE
Work in **back loops** (*see Stitch Guide*) unless otherwise stated.

INSTRUCTIONS
CAP
Note: Thread beads onto yarn, push back until needed.

Row 1: Ch 46, sl st in 2nd ch from hook and in each ch across, turn. (*45 sl sts*)

Row 2: Ch 1, sl st in each st across, leaving last 5 sts unworked for **top of Cap**, turn. (*40 sl sts*)

Row 3: Ch 1, sl st in each sl st across, turn.

Row 4: Ch 1, sl st in each of first 3 sts, pull up 1 bead, [sl st in each of next 3 sts, pull up 1 bead] 4 times, sl st in each of next 20 sts, leaving last 5 sts unworked, turn. (*35 sl sts*)

Row 5: Ch 1, sl st in each sl st across, turn.

Row 6: Ch 1, sl st in each st across, leaving last 10 sts unworked, turn. (*15 sl sts*)

Row 7: Ch 1, sl st in each sl st across, turn.

Row 8: Ch 1, sl st in each of first 5 sts, pull up 1 bead, [sl st in each of next 3 sl sts, pull up 1 bead] 3 times, sl st in each st and in each unworked st across top of Cap, turn. (*45 sl sts*)

Row 9: Ch 1, sl st in each st across, turn.

Rows 10–145: [Rep rows 2–9 consecutively] 17 times.

Rows 146–152: Rep rows 2–8.

Row 153: Hold first and last rows tog, matching sts, sl st tog. Fasten off.

Weave separate strand through rows at top of Cap, pull to gather, secure end.

POMPOM
Wrap yarn around 4 fingers 50 times and remove from fingers, tie separate strand tightly around center of all strands. Cut loops and trim.

Tie Pompom to top of Cap. ■

Unisex Cloche

SKILL LEVEL
◼◼◼◻
INTERMEDIATE

FINISHED SIZES
Instructions given fit 21-inch head circumference (*woman's*); changes for 23-inch head circumference (*man's*) are in [ ].

MATERIALS
- Moda Dea Tweedle Dee bulky (chunky) weight yarn (3½ oz/155 yds/100g per skein):
  1 skein #8917 indigo run (for man's size) or #8906 cinnamon twist (for woman's size)
- TLC Essentials medium (worsted) weight yarn (6 oz/312 yds/170g per skein):
  1 skein #2821 paradise blue (for man's size) or #2919 barn red (for woman's size)
- Sizes H/8/5mm and M/13/9mm crochet hooks or size needed to obtain gauge
- Tapestry needle

GAUGE
Size M hook and bulky yarn: 12 sl sts = 4 inches; 18 sl st rows = 4 inches

PATTERN NOTE
Work in **back loops** (*see Stitch Guide*) unless otherwise stated.

INSTRUCTIONS
CAP
Row 1: With size H hook and medium yarn, ch 6, **change color** (*see Stitch Guide*) to bulky yarn in last ch, with size M hook, ch 21 [23], sl st in 2nd ch from hook and in each of next 19 [21] chs, changing to size H hook and medium yarn in last st, sl st in each of last 6 chs, turn. (*26 [28] sl sts*)

Row 2: Ch 1, sl st in each of first 6 sts, changing to size M hook and bulky yarn in last st, sl st in each st across, leaving last 4 sts unworked for **top of Cap**, turn. (*22 [24] sl sts*)

Row 3: Ch 1, sl st in each of first 16 [18] sts, changing to H hook and medium yarn in last st, sl st in each of last 6 sts, turn.

Row 4: Ch 1, sl st in each of first 6 sts, changing to size M hook and bulky yarn in last st, sl st in each st across, leaving last 4 sts unworked, turn. (*18 [20] sl sts*)

Row 5: Ch 1, sl st in each of first 12 [14] sts, changing to H hook and medium yarn in last st, sl st in each of last 6 sts, turn.

Row 6: Ch 1, sl st in each of first 6 sts, changing to size M hook and bulky yarn in last st, sl st in each of next 12 [14] sts and in next 8 unworked sts across top of Cap, turn. (*26 [28] sl sts*)

Row 7: Ch 1, sl st in each of first 20 [22] sts, changing to H hook and medium yarn in last st, sl st in each of last 6 sts, turn.

Rows 8–91 [8–103]: [Rep rows 2–7 consecutively] 14 [16] times.

Rows 92–96 [104–108]: Rep rows 2–6.

Row 97 [109]: Hold first and last rows tog, matching sts, sl st tog. Fasten off.

Weave separate strand bulky through ends of rows at top of Cap, pull to gather and secure end.◼

Snowball Trim

SKILL LEVEL

INTERMEDIATE

FINISHED SIZE
One size fits most adults: 21-inch circumference

MATERIALS
- SR Kertzers Angel Baby DK light (DK) weight yarn (1¾ oz/ 185 yds/50g per skein): 2 skeins #06 blue
- Size F/5/3.75mm crochet hook or size needed to obtain gauge
- Tapestry needle

GAUGE
24 sl sts = 4 inches; 32 sl st rows = 4 inches

PATTERN NOTE
Work in **back loops** (*see Stitch Guide*) unless otherwise stated.

SPECIAL STITCH
Puff stitch (puff st): Insert hook in next ch sp, pull up long lp, [yo, insert hook in same ch sp, pull up long lp] 3 times, yo, pull through all lps on hook.

INSTRUCTIONS
CAP
Row 1: Ch 51, sl st in 2nd ch from hook and in each ch across, turn. (*50 sl sts*)

Row 2: Ch 1, sl st in each st across, leaving last 5 sts unworked for **top of Cap**, turn. (*45 sl sts*)

Row 3: Ch 1, sl st in each sl st across, turn.

Row 4: Ch 1, sl st in each st across, leaving last 5 sts unworked, turn. (*40 sl sts*)

Row 5: Ch 1, sl st in each sl st across, turn.

Row 6: Ch 1, sl st in each st across, leaving last 5 sts unworked, turn. (*35 sl sts*)

Row 7: Ch 1, sl st in each sl st across, turn.

Row 8: Ch 1, sl st in each sl st across, leaving last 5 sts unworked, turn. (*30 sl sts*)

Row 9: Ch 1, sl st in each sl st across, turn.

Row 10: Ch 1, sl st in each st across, leaving last 5 sts unworked, turn. (*25 sl sts*)

Row 11: Ch 1, sl st in each sl st across, turn.

Row 12: Ch 1, sl st in each st on last row and in each unworked st across top of Cap, turn. (*50 sl sts*)

Row 13: Ch 1, sl st in each st across, turn.

Rows 14–145: [Rep rows 2–13 consecutively] 11 times.

Rows 146–156: Rep rows 2–12.

Row 157: Hold first and last rows tog, matching sts, sl st tog. Fasten off.

Weave separate strand through rows at top of Cap, pull to gather, secure end.

TRIM
Rnd 1: With WS facing, working in ends of rows, join with sc in end of any row between 2 ridges, ch 3, sk next 3 rows, [sc in next row, ch 3, sk next 3 rows] around, join with sl st in beg sc. *(39 ch sps)*

Rnds 2–5: Ch 3, [**puff st** *(see Special Stitch)* in next ch sp, ch 3] around, join with sl st in 3rd ch of beg ch-3.

Rnd 6: Ch 3, [puff st in next ch sp, ch 2] around, join with sl st in 3rd ch of beg ch-3. Fasten off.

Fold up Trim for cuff. ■

Novelty **Cuff**

SKILL LEVEL

INTERMEDIATE

FINISHED SIZE
One size fits most adults: 22-inch circumference

MATERIALS
- Lion Brand Vanna's Choice medium (worsted) weight yarn (3½ oz/ 170 yds/100g per ball): **4 MEDIUM**
    1 ball #107 sapphire
- Lion Brand Lion Bouclé super bulky (super chunky) weight yarn (2½ oz/57 yds/70g per skein): **6 SUPER BULKY**
    1 skein #203 jelly bean
- Size H/8/5mm crochet hook or size needed to obtain gauge
- Tapestry needle

GAUGE
Worsted weight: 17 sl sts = 4 inches; 26 sl st rows = 4 inches

PATTERN NOTE
Work in **back loops** *(see Stitch Guide)* unless otherwise stated.

INSTRUCTIONS
CAP

Row 1: With jelly bean, ch 10, **change color** (*see Stitch Guide*) to sapphire in last ch, ch 36, sl st in 2nd ch from hook and in each of next 34 chs, leaving rem chs unworked for **top of Cap**, turn. (*35 sl sts, 10 chs*)

Row 2: Ch 1, sl st in each of first 30 sts, leaving rems sts unworked, turn. (*30 sl sts*)

Row 3: Ch 1, sl st in each of first 30 sts, changing to jelly bean in last st, sl st in each of next 10 chs from row before last, turn. (*40 sl sts*)

Row 4: Ch 1, sl st in each of first 10 sts, changing to sapphire in last st, sl st in each of next 25 sts, leaving rem sts unworked, turn. (*35 sl sts*)

Row 5: Ch 1, sl st in each of first 25 sts, leaving rem sts unworked, turn. (*25 sl sts*)

Row 6: Ch 1, sl st in each of first 20 sts, leaving rem sts unworked, turn. (*20 sl sts*)

Row 7: Ch 1, sl st in each of first 20 sts, changing to jelly bean in last st, sl st in each of next 10 sts from row before last, turn. (*30 sl sts*)

Row 8: Ch 1, sl st in each of first 10 sts, changing to sapphire in last st, sl st in each of next 15 sts, leaving rem sts unworked, turn. (*25 sl sts*)

Row 9: Ch 1, sl st in each of first 15 sts, leaving rem sts unworked, turn. (*15 sl sts*)

Row 10: Ch 1, sl st in each of first 10 sts, leaving rem sts unworked, turn. (*10 sl sts*)

Row 11: Ch 1, sl st in each of first 10 sts, changing to jelly bean in last st, sl st in each of next 10 sts from row before last, turn. (*20 sl sts*)

Row 12: Ch 1, sl st in each of first 10 sts, changing to sapphire in last st, sl st in each of next 10 sts and in next 25 unworked sts across top of Cap, turn. (*45 sl sts*)

Row 13: Ch 1, sl st in each of first 35 sts, leaving rem sts unworked, turn. (*35 sl sts*)

Rows 14–133: [Rep rows 2–13 consecutively] 10 times.

Rows 134–144: Rep rows 2–12.

Row 145: Hold first and last rows tog, matching sts and changing color as needed, sl st tog. Fasten off.

POMPOM
Wrap jelly bean around 3 fingers 10 times and remove from fingers; tie separate strand of sapphire tightly around center of all strands. Tie Pompom to top of Cap.

Fold up cuff. ∎

Santa Hats

FINISHED SIZES
Adult: 20-inch circumference
Baby: 15-inch circumference

MATERIALS
- Red Heart Soft Yarn medium (worsted) weight yarn (5 oz/ 256 yds/140g per skein): 2 skeins #5142 cherry red
- Red Heart Baby Clouds super bulky (super chunky) weight yarn (6 oz/ 140 yds/170g) per skein): 1 skein #9311 cloud
- Sizes I/9/5.5mm and K/10½/6.5mm crochet hooks or size needed to obtain gauge
- Tapestry needle

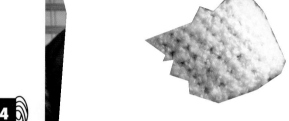

GAUGE
Size I hook: 19 sl sts = 4 inches; 28 sl st rows = 4 inches

PATTERN NOTE
Work in **back loops** (*see Stitch Guide*) unless otherwise stated.

INSTRUCTIONS
ADULT HAT
Row 1: With size I hook and cherry red, ch 101, sl st in 2nd ch from hook and in each ch across, turn. (*100 sl sts*)

Row 2: Ch 1, sl st in each st across, leaving last 10 sts unworked for **top of Hat**, turn. (*90 sl sts*)

Row 3: Ch 1, sl st in each sl st across, turn.

Rows 4–17: [Rep rows 2 and 3 alternately] 7 times. (*20 sl sts at end of last row*)

Row 18: Ch 1, sl st in each st on last row and in each unworked st across top of Hat, turn. (*100 sl sts*)

Row 19: Ch 1, sl st in each st across, turn.

Rows 20–109: [Rep rows 2–19 consecutively] 5 times.

Rows 110–126: Rep rows 2–18.

Row 127: Hold first and last rows tog, matching sts, sl st tog. Fasten off.

TRIM
Rnd 1: With size K hook and cloud, with WS facing, join with sl st in end of any row between 2 ridges, ch 2, evenly sp 33 sc around, placing sts in end of rows between ridges, join with sl st around beg ch 2. (*33 sc*)

Rnds 2–8: Ch 2, sc in each st around, join with sl st around beg ch-2.

Rnds 9 & 10: Ch 2, sc in each of first 16 sts, 2 sc in next st, sc in each st around, join with sl st around beg ch-2. Fasten off at end of last rnd.

POMPOM
Wrap cloud around 3 fingers 10 times. Remove from fingers; tie separate strand of cloud tightly around center of all strands. Tie Pompom to top of Hat.

Fold up Trim for cuff.

BABY HAT
Row 1: With size I hook and cherry red, ch 61, sl st in 2nd ch from hook and in each ch across, turn. *(60 sl sts)*

Row 2: Ch 1, sl st in each st across, leaving last 5 sts unworked for **top of Hat**, turn. *(55 sl sts)*

Row 3: Ch 1, sl st in each sl st across, turn.

Rows 4–19: [Rep rows 2 and 3 alternately] 8 times. *(15 sl sts at end of last row)*

Row 20: Ch 1, sl st in each st on last row and in each unworked st across top of Hat, turn. *(60 sl sts)*

Row 21: Ch 1, sl st in each st across, turn.

Rows 22–81: [Rep rows 2–21 consecutively] 3 times.

Rows 82–100: Rep rows 2–20.

Row 101: Hold first and last rows tog, matching sts, sl st tog. Fasten off.

TRIM
Rnd 1: With size K hook and cloud, with WS facing, join with sl st in end of any row between 2 ridges, ch 2, evenly sp 26 sc around, placing sts in end of rows between ridges, join with sl st around beg ch 2. *(26 sc)*

Rnds 2–6: Ch 2, sc in each st around, join with sl st around beg ch-2. Fasten off at end of last rnd.

POMPOM
Wrap cloud around 3 fingers 10 times. Remove from fingers; tie separate strand of cloud tightly around center of all strands. Tie Pompom to top of Hat.

Fold up Trim for cuff. ■

Stitch Guide

For more complete information, visit **FreePatterns.com**

ABBREVIATIONS

beg	begin/begins/beginning
bpdc	back post double crochet
bpsc	back post single crochet
bptr	back post treble crochet
CC	contrasting color
ch(s)	chain(s)
ch-	refers to chain or space previously made (e.g., ch-1 space)
ch sp(s)	chain space(s)
cl(s)	cluster(s)
cm	centimeter(s)
dc	double crochet (singular/plural)
dc dec	double crochet 2 or more stitches together, as indicated
dec	decrease/decreases/decreasing
dtr	double treble crochet
ext	extended
fpdc	front post double crochet
fpsc	front post single crochet
fptr	front post treble crochet
g	gram(s)
hdc	half double crochet
hdc dec	half double crochet 2 or more stitches together, as indicated
inc	increase/increases/increasing
lp(s)	loop(s)
MC	main color
mm	millimeter(s)
oz	ounce(s)
pc	popcorn(s)
rem	remain/remains/remaining
rep(s)	repeat(s)
rnd(s)	round(s)
RS	right side
sc	single crochet (singular/plural)
sc dec	single crochet 2 or more stitches together, as indicated
sk	skip/skipped/skipping
sl st(s)	slip stitch(es)
sp(s)	space/spaces/spaced
st(s)	stitch(es)
tog	together
tr	treble crochet
trtr	triple treble
WS	wrong side
yd(s)	yard(s)
yo	yarn over

Chain—ch: Yo, pull through lp on hook.

Slip stitch—sl st: Insert hook in st, pull through both lps on hook.

Single crochet—sc: Insert hook in st, yo, pull through st, yo, pull through both lps on hook.

Front post stitch—fp: Back post stitch—bp: When working post st, insert hook from right to left around post st on previous row.

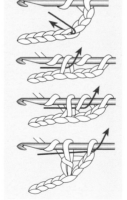

Front loop—front lp Back loop—back lp

Front Loop Back Loop

Half double crochet—hdc: Yo, insert hook in st, yo, pull through st, yo, pull through all 3 lps on hook.

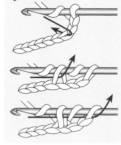

Double crochet—dc: Yo, insert hook in st, yo, pull through st, [yo, pull through 2 lps] twice.

Change colors: Drop first color; with 2nd color, pull through last 2 lps of st.

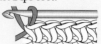

Treble crochet—tr: Yo twice, insert hook in st, yo, pull through st, [yo, pull through 2 lps] 3 times.

Double treble crochet—dtr: Yo 3 times, insert hook in st, yo, pull through st, [yo, pull through 2 lps] 4 times.

Single crochet decrease (sc dec): (Insert hook, yo, draw lp through) in each of the sts indicated, yo, draw through all lps on hook.

Example of 2-sc dec

Half double crochet decrease (hdc dec): (Yo, insert hook, yo, draw lp through) in each of the sts indicated, yo, draw through all lps on hook.

Example of 2-hdc dec

Double crochet decrease (dc dec): (Yo, insert hook, yo, draw loop through, draw through 2 lps on hook) in each of the sts indicated, yo, draw through all lps on hook.

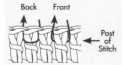

Example of 2-dc dec

Treble crochet decrease (tr dec): Holding back last lp of each st, tr in each of the sts indicated, yo, pull through all lps on hook.

Example of 2-tr dec

US		UK
sl st (slip stitch)	=	sc (single crochet)
sc (single crochet)	=	dc (double crochet)
hdc (half double crochet)	=	htr (half treble crochet)
dc (double crochet)	=	tr (treble crochet)
tr (treble crochet)	=	dtr (double treble crochet)
dtr (double treble crochet)	=	ttr (triple treble crochet)
skip	=	miss

Metric Conversion Charts

METRIC CONVERSIONS

yards	x	.9144	=	metres (m)
yards	x	91.44	=	centimetres (cm)
inches	x	2.54	=	centimetres (cm)
inches	x	25.40	=	millimetres (mm)
inches	x	.0254	=	metres (m)

centimetres	x	.3937	=	inches
metres	x	1.0936	=	yards

INCHES INTO MILLIMETRES & CENTIMETRES (Rounded off slightly)

inches	mm	cm	inches	cm	inches	cm	inches	cm
1/8	3	0.3	5	12.5	21	53.5	38	96.5
1/4	6	0.6	5½	14	22	56	39	99
3/8	10	1	6	15	23	58.5	40	101.5
1/2	13	1.3	7	18	24	61	41	104
5/8	15	1.5	8	20.5	25	63.5	42	106.5
3/4	20	2	9	23	26	66	43	109
7/8	22	2.2	10	25.5	27	68.5	44	112
1	25	2.5	11	28	28	71	45	114.5
1¼	32	3.2	12	30.5	29	73.5	46	117
1½	38	3.8	13	33	30	76	47	119.5
1¾	45	4.5	14	35.5	31	79	48	122
2	50	5	15	38	32	81.5	49	124.5
2½	65	6.5	16	40.5	33	84	50	127
3	75	7.5	17	43	34	86.5		
3½	90	9	18	46	35	89		
4	100	10	19	48.5	36	91.5		
4½	115	11.5	20	51	37	94		

KNITTING NEEDLES CONVERSION CHART

Canada/U.S.	0	1	2	3	4	5	6	7	8	9	10	10½	11	13	15
Metric (mm)	2	2¼	2¾	3¼	3½	3¾	4	4½	5	5½	6	6½	8	9	10

CROCHET HOOKS CONVERSION CHART

Canada/U.S.	1/B	2/C	3/D	4/E	5/F	6/G	8/H	9/I	10/J	10½/K	N
Metric (mm)	2.25	2.75	3.25	3.5	3.75	4.25	5	5.5	6	6.5	9.0

Annie's Attic®

TOLL-FREE ORDER LINE or to request a free catalog (800) LV-ANNIE (800) 582-6643
Customer Service (800) AT-ANNIE (800) 282-6643, **Fax** (800) 882-6643
Visit AnniesAttic.com
We have made every effort to ensure the accuracy and completeness of these instructions.
We cannot, however, be responsible for human error, typographical mistakes or variations in individual work.

ISBN: 978-1-59635-272-8